GREAT YARM[illegible]
and GORLESTON

Front Line Towns

Colin Tooke

First Published 1999
by
Tookes Books
14 Hurrell Road
Caister-on-Sea
Great Yarmouth NR30 5XG

ISBN 0 9532953 1 1

Cover picture - *"The tables groaned with food as the children tucked into more custard and jelly, blancmanges and cakes, tinned peaches and sandwiches than they could ever remember"*
VE celebration party in Gorleston 1945. See page 52.

Printed in England by Blackwell John Buckle
Charles Street, Great Yarmouth, Norfolk

Contents

Introduction		1
1	The Volunteers	3
2	The Air Station	15
3	The Great War	21
4	Second World War	35
5	Naval Bases	53
Acknowledgements and Further Reading		60

The town's first defence against any possible invasion consisted of a flint and brick wall almost one and a quarter miles long and eight metres high enclosing the town on three sides. This picture shows Tower Lane leading from Charles Street to the Friars Tower c1898 by which time houses had been built on and against the wall and the old town had expanded to almost touch the walls, as can be seen by the houses on the right. The cutting through the base of the tower was made early in the 19th century as the town expanded outside the walls. Two thirds of the wall still exists, one of the finest examples of a medieval defensive structure of its type in the country.

Introduction

The town of Great Yarmouth and the adjoining coastline for several miles to the north has always been considered vulnerable to attack by an enemy force in times of conflict. The town has therefore always been in the 'front line' and over the years successive defences have been built to protect it, the harbour and East Anglia from incursion.

The menfolk of the town have, since medieval times, been at the forefront of these defences, both on land and at sea. In the fourteenth century the medieval town was able to provide Admiral John Perebrowne with ships to fight the battle of Sluys, the first great English sea victory, fought off the coast of Holland and later 43 ships and 1075 mariners for the battle of Calais. These events resulted in the town being honoured by having its coat of arms halved with the Royal coat of arms. Throughout the Napoleonic Wars the town was an important naval base and headquarters of the North Sea squadron. It was from Yarmouth that Admiral Duncan and Sir Richard Onslow sailed to win the battle of Camperdown in October 1797, returning to the port with six captured Dutch ships.

Henry III had recognised the important strategic position of Yarmouth in the thirteenth century when he first authorised the townspeople to construct a wall to enclose the town, an impressive defence that was to take 100 years to complete. The wall, much of which survives today, included ten gates and eighteen towers and was to restrict the growth and size of the town for the following four hundred years. A threat of invasion from the Spanish Armada in 1588 led to these defences being strengthened and the town heavily garrisoned. In 1653 a fort, armed with eight cannon, was built on the South Denes to protect the harbour entrance at the commencement of the Dutch Wars. (This building survived until 1832 when it was undermined by the sea and collapsed.) The town once more came back into the front line with two thousand infantry and five troops of cavalry stationed here, the existing defences once again strengthened and improved.

Many military and naval buildings have been erected in the town over the years. One of the earliest was a barracks and small hospital built on the site of an old distillery just outside the town wall, a site which was later to become Grouts Silk Factory, today Sainsburys Supermarket. In 1799 many of the wounded from the battle of Copenhagen were treated at this hospital which was visited by Admiral Lord Nelson on 1 July 1801, his last visit to Norfolk

In 1806 an Armoury was erected on the river side at Southtown to provide arms and equipment for the fleet during the Napoleonic War, one of the cannon barrels from this armoury can be seen today at the north end of the Market Place. In 1809 a Royal Naval Hospital was built on the South Denes and over 600 wounded from the battle of Waterloo were treated there in 1815, many being buried within the grounds. This building, which today is being converted into residential units, was to take on several military and naval roles during the nineteenth century, including at one time being the only Naval Lunatic Asylum in the country.

The wall plaque that still exists at the old Naval Hospital indicating the last resting place of several soldiers and sailors treated there in the early nineteenth century.

Towards the end of the eighteenth century there were renewed threats of invasion with the outbreak of the American War. (The Dutch and French joined the American colonies and Yarmouth remembered that Holland was only 95 miles away.) The medieval town wall had fallen into disrepair and was obsolete as a defence and in 1801 three gun batteries, equipped with 32-pounders, were constructed on the Denes together with a small stockaded battery on Gorleston cliffs. These became known as the South Star Battery (on land that is today the southern end of Harbord Crescent), the Town Battery (later to be the site of the Royal Aquarium) and the North Star Battery (today Blake Road and Collingwood Road). The Town Battery was demolished in 1859 but the North and South Batteries were rebuilt and re-equipped, remaining operational until the end of the century. With its obsolete weapons the South Battery was to become the town's only defence at the outbreak of the First World War in 1914.

The Volunteers

From the middle of the nineteenth century military forces were recruited to form an army reserve, men who could be called up for service at any time and serve where and when the regular army required. When not required they were 'disembodied' and sent home, but liable to be called up again at any time. Each year these men were required to complete at least fifty-six days training. This force, the Militia, was recruited throughout the country and paid by the government. A few years later another force, the Volunteers, was recruited. These men received very little pay and had to provide their own uniforms and equipment. They were all local men, recruited at a time when the government had no money to pay additional forces but needed them for national defence.

In 1853 the Norfolk Artillery Militia was formed with its headquarters at Yarmouth, most of the men coming from the East and West Norfolk Infantry Militia, a force already in existence. The following year new barracks were built for these men on land south of the Naval Hospital (see above engraving dated 27 July 1863). During their training periods the Militia used the North and South Batteries for gun practice. The old Armoury at Southtown was also brought back into use, this time as a Barracks. The Russian Wars saw many of these men join the regular army and serve in the Crimea. The town received two trophies from this war, 36-pounder bronze Russian guns that were first placed outside the old Town Hall and later moved to the Jetty.

In 1859 the 'Volunteers' was formed, consisting of two companies, the Rifle Volunteers and the Artillery Volunteers. These had soon recruited 100 men apiece and the Artillery was given the use of the South Battery for their training sessions while the Rifles had the use of a Rifle Range on the North Denes. Each summer both the North and South Denes were occupied by either the Militia or the Volunteers carrying out their training and annual inspections as well as companies of up to 3000 men from other parts of the country using the area for their annual camps. All this military activity brought financial benefit to the town as many thousands of spectators came to witness the reviews and mock battles held on the Denes, events which were to continue until the end of the century.

In 1867 the Riflc Volunteers raised £1,300 to build a new Drill Hall on St Peter's Plain, fronting York Road, and later the Artillery Volunteers were able to build themselves a Drill Hall on land off Nelson Road, now known as Artillery Square. Both these buildings still exist. Royal Naval Volunteers was formed in 1886 and was equipped with a gun platform and a drill shed on the North Denes near the Battery. Nelson Road was extended by 200 yards to improve access to the North Battery and Naval Gun Sheds, an extension that was later named North Denes Road.

In 1871 HRH the Prince of Wales (later Edward VII) became the Honorary Colonel of the Militia and the following year paid his first of many visits to Yarmouth, staying at the Shadingfield Lodge. The company soon became known as the Prince of Wales Own Norfolk Artillery Militia. The Barracks now covered an area of 21 acres and in 1883 the Assembly Rooms on Marine Parade (now the Masonic Club) was purchased as the Officers' Mess.

Soldiers on bicycles became a reality in 1893 with the formation of Cyclist Companies within the Volunteers. Useful in areas susceptible to invasion they could patrol the coastline and also act as a holding force until the main army arrived. At Yarmouth the 2nd Volunteer Battalion, Norfolk Regiment, was formed.

NOTICE

SOUTH DENES.

VOLUNTEER ENCAMPMENT

The Norfolk Volunteers will be encamped on the South Denes, from the 22nd to the 31st of the present month, and the Worshipful the Mayor suggests that Fishing Boat Owners should not spread their nets on the South Denes, during that time.

BY ORDER,

T. M. BAKER,

Town Clerk.

TOWN CLERK'S OFFICES, *July* 15*th*, 1880.
GREAT YARMOUTH.

COOPER & SON, STEAM PRINTERS, YARMOUTH.

The South Denes was a popular site for both Volunteer and Militia summer camps and this poster issued in July 1880 gives notice to fishermen that their traditional net drying grounds would not be available during the military encampment. The Racecourse was also on the South Denes at this time but the land had little other use except for military training and the fishing industry. Many people would visit the town to view the large encampments and watch the mock battles and manoeuvres.

The Boer War in 1900 saw many members of both the Militia and the Volunteers going to South Africa, some being repatriated the following year and receiving a hero's welcome when they arrived back at Vauxhall Station. Both the North and South Denes continued to be used by large numbers of troops for annual training and summer camps until an Army reorganisation took place in 1908. The Militia then became part of a national Special Reserve force and lost its close identity with the town. The Officers' Mess was sold and the regimental silver and furniture auctioned, only the wooden shields with the family arms of the officers of the Regiment which had decorated the Officers' Mess remaining. Today 73 of these shields remain in the Masonic Club, a unique collection of nineteenth century militaria. The South Denes Barracks continued in government ownership until finally sold to the Corporation in 1924 and the houses known as the Barrack Estate were built on the site. The only military building to survive today is the house at the rear of the Rok public house (previously the Gunner). Battery Road survives, once a track leading to the South Battery as does Barrack Road which originally led from the quay to the western entrance of the Military Barracks.

The Volunteer forces also ceased to exist in 1908, becoming the new Army Territorial Force. The York Road Drill Hall was now used by the Great Yarmouth detachments of the 5th and 6th Battalions Norfolk Regiment (the 6th being a cyclist company) and the Artillery Square Drill Hall used by the Royal Field Artillery, 1st Norfolk Battery.

On the North Denes the naval gun platform and drill shed were removed in 1912 and the 1920s saw the removal of the North Battery and the rifle range.

One of the pair of Russian guns captured at Sevastopol during the Crimea War. First brought to the town in 1857 they stood outside the old Town Hall until 1880 when they were moved to the Jetty. They remained here until the Second World War when they were taken for scrap metal to help the war effort.

Men of the Norfolk Rifle Volunteers in camp at Yarmouth c1870.
This is thought to be the earliest military photograph taken in Norfolk showing local men in uniform. The uniforms are grey with blue piping and at this period there were no cap badges.

The Militia Barracks was built in 1855 on land between the Naval Hospital and the South Battery. This picture shows the main barrack block, the first part to be built. The roadway at the bottom of the picture would today be Dickens Avenue, earlier known as Quarter Mile Road. The Greenacre School was built on part of the site of the building shown here in 1929. The houses which now form the Barrack Estate were built on the remainder of the military land after the Corporation bought it from the government in 1924.

The South Star battery c1860. In 1858 the Batteries had been repaired and re-equipped with larger 68-pounders. In the background can be seen the Wellington Pier, opened in 1853 and the Victoria Hotel.

Men of the Norfolk Artillery Militia assembled at the South Battery c1880. This Battery was used by both the Militia and the Volunteer Artillery for practice sessions when shot and shells were fired at targets placed in the roadstead. The guns were replaced several times over the years until eventually 100-pounders were installed. In this picture shells can be seen stacked near the magazines, replacing the round shot seen in the picture above.

Men of the Prince of Wales Own Norfolk Artillery Militia grouped around an 80-pounder at the South Star Battery c1880.

Men of the 2nd Volunteer Battalion Norfolk Regiment c1890. The uniform consists of red tunics with white collar and cuffs and dark navy trousers with a thin red pinstripe. The buttons and belt buckle were of white metal denoting they were Volunteers, only the regular army had brass buttons and buckles. Some of these men would have seen service in the Boer War (1899-1902).

A military camp on the South Denes before 1882.
Each bell tent would accommodate 12 men sleeping with their feet towards the centre pole. In front of the camp can be seen the white railings of the Race Course which until 1920 was on the South Denes. These large military summer camps were very popular with sightseers and horse brakes, one of which can be seen to the right of the picture, which would take people from the seafront and the town centre to view the camp. A Jarrolds Guide of Great Yarmouth dated 1896, describing the South Denes said, "In the summer months a Grand Field Day of the Volunteers is held here as the Denes possess very great facilities for the exercise of military tactics. The grounds are also used for the encampment of brigades of Volunteers from a considerable distance."

Among the many fishing boats seen in the picture are YH442 *'Alice'*, a small 39 ton trawling smack built in 1869 sailing down river while moored on the Gorleston bank is YH49 *'Alpha'*, a 73 ton trawling smack built in 1876 and one of the Hewett fleet based at Gorleston.

The Royal Naval Hospital, Queens Road, opened in 1811. It later became a Naval Barracks with Captain George Manby, better known for his life saving apparatus, as barrack-master. The building became a Military Hospital again at the outbreak of the war with Russia and in 1863 transferred back to the Admiralty for use as a Naval Lunatic Asylum. From 1939 until 1945 it was the Naval Base *HMS Watchful* (see chapter 4).

Southtown Road c1885. On the right is the entrance to the Barracks, originally built as an Armoury for use throughout the Napoleonic Wars. The two cannon barrels mark the entrance, one of which can be seen today outside the Fishermen's Hospital in the Market Place.

The Assembly Rooms was built in 1863 and from 1879 until 1908 was the Officers' Mess for the Norfolk Militia Artillery. Today the building is the Masonic Lodge.

Regimental silver set out for a dinner in the Assembly Rooms in 1891 when it was the Officers' Mess. The shields bearing the family arms of the officers of the Regiment can be seen decorating the walls of the Mess, many of these wooden shields still exist in the Masonic Lodge.

Colonel HRH The Prince of Wales seated in the centre of this picture with the officers of the Prince of Wales Own Norfolk Artillery. Taken outside the Shadingfield Lodge in 1899.

Officers and Senior NCOs of the 3rd Volunteer Battalion Norfolk Regiment in camp on the South Denes c1907. This was a transitional period for the army hence the variety of uniforms worn by men of the same Regiment.

Crowds awaiting the return of the Great Yarmouth Volunteer Artillery on North Quay 18 May 1901. The Volunteers arrived at Vauxhall Station on their return from the Boer War. Every available viewpoint is used, even the girders of the railway bridge in the background.

Accompanied by the band of the Prince of Wales Own Norfolk Artillery Militia the Volunteers march along North Quay en route to the Town Hall and a reception by the Mayor. Shops and businesses were temporarily closed and an enormous crowd welcomed the men back from their service in South Africa.

The Air Station

The Royal Flying Corps was formed on 13 April 1912 with a Naval and a Military Wing. The Naval Wing, under the direction of the Admiralty, decided to form a chain of 'flying stations' along the east coast and subsequently a site on the South Denes at Great Yarmouth was identified as being suitable. The general requirements for a hydro-aeroplane station, as these sites were known, were an area of land of at least 5 acres with a sheltered shore frontage in the proximity of, or adjacent to, land suitable for an aerodrome. There should be a harbour close at hand and suitable accommodation for housing personnel. Great Yarmouth met all these requirements, land on the eastern edge of the South Denes having the shore frontage and adequate accommodation being available at the Coastguard Station on Marine Parade for the expected 2 officers and 20 men. The aircraft that were under development at this time were largely experimental and most had to be launched from a slipway, the harbour being required for the motor boats which assisted the machines, an essential part of these early naval air stations. One land machine was also to be based here, the open Denes to the south of Nelson's column being considered suitable as a landing ground.

The station was commissioned on 15 April 1913 and the official headquarters was established in the town at 25 Regent Street (until recently the office of the Great Yarmouth Mercury). The first machine to arrive was a land biplane and flew in from Hendon on 31 May, a military biplane with a maximum speed of 54 miles per hour. This arrival created great interest in the town and it was hoped that it would add to the attractions for summer visitors. A few days after the arrival of the biplane some of the town dignitaries were taken for short flights, a good public relations exercise.

As the air station developed, hangars and other buildings were erected, two slipways built and the site fenced off. The word 'seaplane' was officially introduced to replace 'hydro-aeroplane' and by July three machines had arrived. The station was now able to take part in the important naval manoeuvres held that month, the first time aircraft were used by the Royal Navy in conjunction with the fleet at sea. These manoeuvres were to be a prelude to the forthcoming events of 1914-18.

At the outbreak of war in August 1914 the role of the Great Yarmouth air station was mainly coastal patrol, covering an area from Cromer to Southwold. The first air raid on this country (detailed in the next chapter) happened on 19 January 1915 when two German Naval Zeppelin airships crossed the North Sea and slowly passed over East Anglia, dropping bombs on Great Yarmouth, Sheringham and King's Lynn. Although there were three machines at the air station they were not able to attack the airships, they were incapable of reaching the height at which the airships could cruise and the only armament they carried was one rifle in the hands of the pilot. Not a single round was fired from any gun at these airships throughout the raid.

As Zeppelin raids increased over the following months so did the development of the aircraft and their weapons. Machine guns were carried and incendiary darts developed, designed to be dropped on an airship, puncturing the fabric and setting it on fire. The first Zeppelin to be destroyed by a machine from the Yarmouth air station was on 27 November 1916 when the L21 was set on fire, falling into the sea off Lowestoft. The station now had over 30 machines and considerable improvements were being made regarding armament and reliability. A flying boat based at Yarmouth (No 8666) had the distinction of being the first to destroy an enemy airship and through later missions became the most famous flying boat in the service. Throughout the war the station played an important role in submarine detection and the destruction of enemy airships.

On 5 August 1918 thirteen aircraft took off from Yarmouth to intercept a Zeppelin raid, one piloted by Major Cadbury with Captain Leckie in the rear seat. They encountered a Zeppelin 40 miles NE of Yarmouth and attacked at 16,400 feet, Leckie firing an explosive bullet into the airship, setting it on fire. For this action both men were awarded the Distinguished Flying Cross.

In 1918 the Royal Naval Air Service and the Royal Flying Corps became united as the Royal Air Force. When the war was over it was decided that the Yarmouth air station was not to be permanent and the staff and machines were slowly dispersed to other sites. The final pieces of equipment were taken away in January 1920 and the station closed. During its short life the Yarmouth air station played an important role in the development of aircraft and air warfare. Many brave and heroic airmen flew from it, contributing much towards the town's military history.

An aerial view of the Naval Air Station on the South Denes in 1918. The two slipways for launching the sea planes can be seen together with the hangars and sheds of the station. Several planes can be seen on the Denes in the foreground which was the airfield.

Hangars and workshops of the Air Station c1916. Most of these buildings were removed soon after the station closed in 1920 but one has survived until today, although in a dilapidated state, as the only physical reminder of this once important complex. The Yarmouth Air Station became a base for aeroplanes, seaplanes and flying-boats during the six years it was operational.

The first flying machine to arrive at Yarmouth was this Maurice Farman 'Longhorn' with a 70 hp Renault engine. This aircraft had a maximum speed of 54 mph and was built at Hendon.

A Short Seaplane with a 100 bhp Gnome engine. This 1914 machine had two seats with the pilot in front and the observer behind. Only one of these machines was based at Yarmouth. As can be seen from this picture launching and recovering these early 'hydro-aeroplanes' was a difficult and labour intensive exercise.

The funeral procession for Flight Sub. Lieutenant G.W. Hilliard in St Peter's Road, September 1915. Hilliard was the first war casualty of the Yarmouth Air Station having crash landed at Bacton while flying a two-hour patrol between Lowestoft and Cromer. On landing the undercarriage of his machine collapsed and the bombs he was carrying exploded.

Ground personnel at the Air Station standing in front of a Sopwith Pup. In the early days of the station the only armament a plane had was a rifle on the pilot's lap.

Ground personnel with a Short Seaplane in front of the North Hangar at the Air Station in 1916. By this period machine guns had been developed which were able to fire through the propellers, a great advancement in aerial warfare.

The Great War

War was declared at midnight on 3 August 1914, at the height of the holiday season. For several years the German High Seas Fleet had been increasing in strength and this now imposed a real threat to the 'front line' coastal towns facing the North Sea. Talk of an invasion was rife and the complete lack of defences along the coast from the Wash to the Thames left the coastline open to attack. At Great Yarmouth the only defence was an obsolete and useless battery of antiquated muzzle loading guns on the South Denes. The authorities made every effort to assure the public that there was no danger to the East Coast and no need for anyone to cancel holiday bookings or curtail their stay in the town. This assurance however had a limited effect and there was a rapid exodus of holidaymakers from the town.

When it was realised that the war would not be over in a matter of weeks the fortification of the coastline began. Lord Kitchener made his appeal for men to join his 'New Army' in mid August and enthusiasm linked to patriotism encouraged many able bodied men to join up. The town soon became an important Naval Submarine base with *HMS Adamant* stationed at South Quay as the depot ship. The fishing industry was suspended and many of the town's fishermen volunteered for the Trawler Section of the Royal Naval Reserve, at first carrying out minesweeping duties but later engaged in submarine hunting and convoy protection work.

In November a blackout was imposed in coastal towns which in Yarmouth meant that street lighting was forbidden on any road which could be seen from the sea and the tram service along the Marine Parade was curtailed after dark. The following year the Easter Fair was only allowed open during the hours of daylight and the edges of kerbs on street corners were painted white to assist pedestrians. Many public buildings were turned over to military use, the Volunteer Training Corps using the Winter Garden, Pier Gardens, Wellesley and Gorleston Recreation Grounds for drill purposes and Gorleston Pavilion becoming a canteen and recreation room for troops stationed in the town.

The first time the war really touched Yarmouth was on 3 November 1914 when the town was shelled by a force of seven German cruisers and attendant destroyers at 7am. No damage was done and the shells fell harmlessly on the beach but this was the first attack made on this country by a hostile force for almost 250 years, enough to convince many people the time had come to evacuate the town. Two more bombardments followed later in the war, one on 25 April 1915 when some damage was sustained and a more serious attack on 14 January 1918 when 50 shells hit the town within five minutes, killing four people and injuring eight.

Following the first attack the coastal defences were strengthened and the coastline from Mundesley to Yarmouth was patrolled by an armoured train, constructed using two 12-pound naval guns and a machine gun, mounted on wagons with an armour plated locomotive located in the middle. Although this train patrolled the line as far as Yarmouth Beach station until the end of the war it did so without ever firing a shot. By 1917 the coastal fortifications were more substantial and included a 4.7-inch naval gun installed on Gorleston cliffs to cover the approach to the harbour and a 15-pounder at Caister. A series of trenches and pillboxes were built (two of which still survive on either side of the Acle New Road just outside the town).

On 19 January 1915 the unexpected happened when at 8.30pm a Zeppelin airship of the German Navy slowly passed over the town and dropped ten bombs, the first time England had been subjected to an aerial attack. The bombs fell in a line from Albemarle Road to the South Denes but it was the one which fell on St Peter's Plain which caused the most damage and produced the first two deaths in England by bombs from the air. St Peter's Villa was the house which took the main blast and the casualties were Martha Taylor, a 72 year old lady who lived nearby and Samuel Smith, a 53 year old shoemaker of 44 York Road. Another bomb fell outside the First and Last Tavern on Southgate Road and considerable damage was caused by a bomb which fell on the Fish Wharf near the Fish Wharf Refreshment Rooms (now the Dolphin public house).

The exodus of men into the forces brought hardship to the town as the male workforce quickly diminished. The financial distress arising from the effect of the war on the holiday and fishing industries was eased in 1917 when government aid was granted to 'The East Coast Watering Places' and Yarmouth declared a Depressed Area. Near starvation conditions now existed for many people in the town. A compensation scheme was also now in place for property damaged in air raids or bombardments.

St George's Mens Service was a club for young men who met at St George's Rooms, King Street. By 1917 over half of the club members (326) had joined the services and to keep them in touch with home a monthly newsletter was compiled. Here the club leader Mr Whitehead (in the centre of the picture) is seen printing the newsletter at his home 78 Wolseley Road. This thriving club ran for many years after the war.

By April 1917 food rationing had been introduced and the shortage of food meant compulsory use of land for cultivation of crops. The flower beds in the Wellington Gardens and other parts of the town were sown with potatoes as were 22 acres of other land in the Borough and land on the Racecourse in front of the grandstand. This was the most depressing year of the war, large casualty lists appeared in local papers, there was a shortage of goods in the shops and wages were frozen. Bread cost 5¼d a loaf, sausages 1s (5p) a pound while a conductor on the trams earned 21s (£1.05) a week. The summer season, albeit somewhat curtailed, managed to continue through the war years but the government had prohibited the annual Autumn Herring Fishery, this causing great hardship in a town where many hundreds of families depended on the fishing industry for their livelihood.

On 11 November 1918 Germany admitted defeat and signed an armistice which came into effect four days later when church bells rang out and a war-weary country celebrated Victory Day.

The German Naval Zeppelin L3 which bombed Yarmouth on 19 January 1915.
Airships such as these had a top speed of around 50 mph and could climb to 5,000 feet.

Crewed by 16 men, commanded by Kapitan-Leutnant Fritz and armed with 8 explosive bombs and 10 crude incendiary devices this airship had left Fuhlsbuttel, just north of Hamberg, at 10.45am. It crossed the coastline near Happisburgh about 7.40pm and turned towards Yarmouth. A 22lb incendiary bomb was dropped when the airship was over Ormesby, falling harmlessly into a field. A few minutes later the L3 was over the town and at 8.30pm dropped what was to be the first explosive bomb on England. It took the airship ten minutes to pass over the town in a north/south direction and people gathered in the streets in groups to watch it pass over, not considering there could be any danger.

The picture on the left shows part of a 110lb explosive bomb thrown from the L3 over the town.

KEEP THIS IN A PROMINENT PLACE.

Directions to the Public in the event of Bombardment or Invasion.

In case of BOMBARDMENT do NOT go into the STREET, but ***keep*** in your cellar or ***on the ground floor of your home.***

In case of a hostile landing and the necessity arising of leaving the town, VEHICLES from ***YARMOUTH*** must travel by CAISTER ROAD.

FOOT PASSENGERS from Yarmouth must proceed past VAUXHALL STATION on to the ACLE NEW ROAD.

Both Vehicles and Foot Passengers from ***SOUTHTOWN AND GORLESTON*** must use the road to ST. OLAVES via BRADWELL AND ASHBY.

It must be borne in mind that in case of any of the roads being required for the movement of Troops, civilians must be prepared to move off the roads temporarily into adjacent fields if necessary in order that they may not hinder the movement of the Troops.

Persons leaving the town should provide themselves with ***food*** and ***warm clothing.***

If you wish for ***advice*** ask one of the SPECIAL CONSTABLES who will be on duty in case of danger, and be prepared to obey the directions given to you.

If any alarm comes during school hours, the ***children attending the elementary schools*** will be sent home at once.

DAVID McCOWAN,
Mayor.

TOWN HALL,
GREAT YARMOUTH.
6th February, 1915.

A handbill issued to the inhabitants of the town in 1915 giving instructions on what to do if there was an invasion or bombardment. At a later date in the war the dykes on the Southtown marshes were bridged to enable quicker and safer evacuation from the town.

10772 18 THE GERMAN AIR RAID ON GREAT YARMOUTH, JANUARY 19th, 1915. ROTARY PHOTO. E.C.
MR ELLIS WOUNDED BY A BOMB, AND HIS RUINED HOUSE, AT LANCASTER ROAD CORNER ST. PETER'S PLAIN.

The fourth bomb dropped by the Zeppelin L3 was the one which caused the most damage that night. This postcard shows St Peter's Villa with the occupier Mr Ellis standing outside. Mr Ellis happened to be in the rear of the house when the front was blown out thereby escaping with minor wounds. Not so lucky was Martha Taylor who lived at No 2, she was found in the road, her clothes torn off and part of one of her arms laying near her. Almost in the same place was found the body of Samuel Smith of 44 York Road, laying in a pool of blood with part of his head blown off. Mr Smith was a shoemaker whose shop was close to where the bomb fell and it appears he had been standing outside his shop, no doubt watching the Zeppelin with curiosity.

These two unfortunate people had become the first to be killed in this country by an air raid.

10772–15 THE GERMAN AIR RAID ON GREAT YARMOUTH, JANUARY 19th, 1915. ROTARY PHOTO. E.C.
DAMAGED HOUSES AT ST. PETER'S PLAIN.

The postcard shows further damage to property in the area, described by a local reporter the following day as "a scene of considerable ruin". St Peter's Villa was rebuilt after the war and now displays a plaque saying "The first house in Great Britain to be damaged by a Zeppelin Air Raid 19 January 1915".

Windows were broken in property covering a wide area including Drake's Buildings, York Road and Lancaster Road. St Peter's church, seen in the postcard on the right did not escape damage. The injured at the scene were treated by local doctor Dr Leonard Ley who also went down in history as the first surgeon to operate on an air raid victim when he removed a bomb splinter from the chest of a soldier wounded at the eastern end of St Peter's church. Dr Ley had the splinter mounted as a tie pin.

As the Zeppelin continued its path across the town it dropped further bombs including one on the Fishwharf area. This damaged the Port and Haven Commissioners salt water tank, brought down an electric lamp standard and burst a water main. The worst damage was done to the Fishwharf Refreshment Rooms (today the Dolphin). This was owned by the Corporation at that time and they estimated the damage at £200.

10772–14 ROTARY PHOTO, E.C.
THE GERMAN AIR RAID ON GREAT YARMOUTH, JANUARY 19th, 1915.
DAMAGE DONE TO ST. PETER'S CHURCH.

The Fishwharf Refreshment Rooms, damaged on 19 January 1915. Joseph Steele was licensee at the time and is quoted by the local paper as saying, "the terrible force of the explosion is easily demonstrated when I tell you that one picture hanging on the wall of my drawing room was turned face to the wall by the shock"!

Bomb damage to the Fishwharf Post Office 19 January 1915. This Post Office was only used during the autumn fishing season. From here a pneumatic tube ran underground to the main Post Office on Hall Quay for the transmission of telegrams, probably the longest pneumatic tube in the country.

Men of the National Reservists from the Artillery Drill Hall with part of an unexploded bomb dropped by the Zeppelin on 19 January 1915.
This bomb fell at the rear of 78 Crown Road (near Gordon Terrace)

Men of the Great Yarmouth Volunteer Training Corps being inspected in front of the Royal Aquarium 28 February 1915. The VTC was set up in 1914 and was the equivalent of the Second World War Home Guard. Each man has a VTC badge on his coat.

The cyclists of the Volunteer Training Corps ready for inspection 28 February 1915.

A detachment of the 6th Battalion Norfolk Regiment (Cyclists) at Yarmouth c1915.

These men were responsible for coastal patrol from Wells to Gorleston. Men joining the Territorial Cyclists had to be aged 17 to 35, be at least 5′2″ tall and possess their own cycle. They became known as the 'Gaspipe Cavalry'. The Battalion was disbanded in 1918 when new military technology superseded the need for soldiers on bicycles.

The picture on the left shows the gutted remains of the Cliff Hotel at Gorleston being guarded by armed guards following the disastrous fire on Boxing Day 1915. The hotel had been taken over by the military and was being used to billet soldiers.

The Cliff Hotel had been built in 1898 and had 139 bedrooms. It was visited by the Prince of Wales in 1899.

The Auxiliary Hospital of the British Red Cross Society and St John Ambulance was opened on 29 November 1914 at 'Seafield', a large house on the corner of King's Road and Nelson Road. It provided accommodation for 37 patients and by the end of the war had treated 815 people. The house is now known as Seafield Court.

In the drive to promote War Saving Certificates the Mayor, Alderman Worlledge, is seen here addressing a large crowd on Hall Quay in 1917. Although an aeroplane has been brought from the Air Station the town did not have a real tank and had to improvise with a tram cleverly disguised to resemble one. It was even given a number YH777, similar to a fishing boat, to add a local flavour to the appeal.

A 20 ton tank, named Kiwi, was given to the town in 1919 by the National Savings Committee. The tank is seen here with the official reception committee before it was placed on its plinth at the south east corner of Hall Quay.

Hall Quay in 1925. The tank is hidden behind the trees on the right. In 1929 work started to change the road layout in preparation for the new bridge and the tank was taken away for scrap in June of that year.

Peace celebrations were held in the Borough on 18 and 19 July 1919 and began with a dinner on Friday 18 July for all discharged, demobilised and serving members of the forces on leave and all Boy Scouts with war service. To accommodate this large number of people the dinner was held at eight locations, Goode's Rooms, The Drill Halls at York Road and Nelson Road, Savoy Hotel, Hill's Restaurant, Arcade Restaurant, Gorleston Pavilion and the Town Hall. At each venue after dinner entertainment was arranged and during the evening the Mayor and Mayoress visited each group. On Saturday there was a Car and Trade Cart Procession through the town followed by a Firework Display on the beach. All the pensioners in the town received a special grant of 2s 6d (12p).

Price 3d.

County Borough of

Great Yarmouth.

Peace Celebrations

JULY 18th & 19th, 1919.

Souvenir Programme.

The Mayor, Alderman Harbord, watches the Town Clerk read the official Peace Proclamation outside the Town Hall on 28 June 1919. The ceremony included sheathing the 17th century Sword of Justice (seen on the Clerk's left), part of the town regalia only taken out of its sheath during times of war.

On 31 July 1919 a German submarine, the Deutschland, was towed into the port. Built in 1916 the submarine had been bought by the publishers Horatio Bottomley after the war and was used to advertise the magazine John Bull.

The memorial to the 1,472 local men killed in the Great War was unveiled in St George's Park on 7 January 1922 by HRH Prince Henry (later to become the Duke of Gloucester).

The Second World War

In 1939, at the beginning of the second major conflict of the century, the town of Great Yarmouth once again found itself firmly in the front line. As on previous occasions an invasion was thought likely and in 1939 precautions against such an event were well in hand. The beaches were heavily mined and lined with barbed wire, the Britannia Pier had a large gap blown in it to impede the landing of any vehicles and all access to the seafront was barred by street barricades. Tank traps were constructed along the beaches to the north of the town and new pillboxes were built (many of which still exist) to supplement those still existing from the previous war. These, together with a system of trenches and road blocks, formed a defensive line around the town from Caister Road to the Acle New Road and along the line of the railway to Lowestoft. The summer season of 1939 was cut short in August and all centres of entertainment were closed on instructions from the Government. The fishing industry, still not fully recovered from the disruption of only twenty years earlier, was again closed down.

Added to the threat of invasion was the possibility of air raids and gas attacks, gas masks being issued to everyone, including children, these having to be carried at all times. Schools in the town were closed until the necessary shelters had been built and in open spaces all over the town public air raid shelters were under construction. An Air Raid Precaution system, the ARP, had been prepared as early as 1937 and was now implemented, Wardens were appointed and in the event of a public siren being sounded the Wardens would patrol their various sectors of the town and report any 'incident' to the Control Centre (the Art School on Trafalgar Road) from where the emergency services were co-ordinated.

During the first three days of September 1939 over 7000 people, mainly women and children, arrived from the London area by steamers, staying in the town a few days before being transferred by road to safer inland areas. Many people were evacuated from the town itself in the early years of the war, reducing the population to almost a third of its pre-war figure.

Once again gun batteries were constructed to protect the harbour and beaches. Three new batteries were built, the North Battery at the junction of Jellicoe Road and North Drive, armed with two 6-inch ex-naval guns and two searchlights while another battery was built at the harbour mouth on the end of the South Pier. The third, on Gorleston Cliffs and known as the Links Battery, was the largest, equipped with two 6-inch guns and two searchlights. The surrounding bungalows provided the living accommodation, stores and officers' mess for the personnel who manned the battery. In addition to these main batteries anti-aircraft guns were placed at strategic points around the town, including one on Stonecutters Quay and several along the sea front. A new Drill Hall had been built in 1938 on the west side of Southtown Road, almost opposite the old Barracks and Armoury, by the Royal Artillery. This was now used as a depot for heavy anti-aircraft guns which were moved to their locations by a detachment of RASC transporters also based there. The Observer Corps also used this building as an information centre, a building which in more recent years was used by Hughes Electrical.

The vast network of waterways to the west of the town was not left unprotected. A flotilla of twenty-six small motor boats, requisitioned from holiday hire companies, was used to patrol the rivers and broads, ready to intercept any seaplanes which might attempt a 'landing'.

The last three months of 1939 and the first few months of 1940 was a period known as the 'phoney war'. Rationing, the blackout and general austerity were constant reminders that a war was in progress but to many people it seemed a distant and political war. This was soon to change however with the first air raid on the town at 6.30am on 11 July 1940. No air raid siren sounded as a single plane, flying out of low cloud over the sea, dropped bombs on the junction of Gordon Road and Wolseley Road, Southtown. Two houses in Gordon Road received direct hits resulting in four people being killed and another three injured. This was the first time the ARP services had been called into action and a first-aid party from the Cobholm post attended with an ambulance from Watsons garage and a rescue squad of six men. This was to be the first of over ninety air raids the town had to endure before the war was over, more than any other coastal town in the country.

The year 1941 was the worst year of the war for Great Yarmouth. Frequent air raids, during which over 7000 incendiary bombs and 800 high explosive bombs were dropped, killed 109 people and destroyed a lot of property. The most severe of these raids began just after midnight on 8 April when 4000 incendiary bombs were dropped over an area from the Market Place, across the Rows to the South Quay. By 2am fire fighting assistance was being requested from units as far afield as Norwich and Cromer to help with the 65 major fires and 200 smaller fires the bombs had caused. Over 400 people were made homeless and many well known shops including Marks & Spencer, Hill's Restaurant, and Boots Chemist were destroyed or seriously damaged. The resulting casualties from this night of destruction were 17 killed and 68 injured.

Air raids continued throughout 1941 causing considerable damage both in Yarmouth and Gorleston. One of the town's famous attractions, the Revolving Tower north of the Britannia Pier, was demolished in 1941 as it was thought to serve as a landmark for enemy planes.

During 1942, although there were fewer air raids, the destruction continued. On 25 June incendiary bombs destroyed the Parish Church, only the shell remaining at daybreak. Since a very high proportion of the buildings within the Town Wall dated from the seventeenth century it was inevitable that a number of buildings of historic interest would be damaged.

Low flying aircraft became a problem in 1943 and Barrage Balloons appeared over the town. These large silver coloured balloons were anchored in open spaces such as St Georges park. During a raid on 11 May 1943 on the north end of the town 49 people were killed and 41 injured. In this total were 26 ATS girls who had just returned to their quarters on North Drive when it received a direct hit.

By 1944 air raids were considerably reduced and evacuees returned to the town. Repairs to damaged property began and the Council bought land at Gorleston for new housing (the Magdalen College Estate) and temporary prefab houses on the Shrublands Estate. The Home Guard was stood down on 3 December 1944 and finally hostilities in Europe came to an end on 8 May 1945. Post-war recovery began and a limited programme of summer attractions was arranged for the 1945 season with 'Showtime' at the Wellington Pier opening on 30 June.

The long task of clearing the beaches began and the central beach was opened to the public in July although no deckchair or tent hire concessions were allowed. Once again the town had survived an attack, this time most definitely in the 'front line'.

Air Raid Precautions

IMPORTANT

Notice to Householders

WARNING OF AIR RAIDS will be given by a fluctuating or warbling signal of varying pitch or a succession of intermittent blasts sounded by hooters and sirens. These signals may be supplemented by sharp blasts on whistles.

The " RAIDERS PASSED " signal will be a continuous signal at a steady pitch.

PUBLIC SHELTERS & TRENCHES

It should be clearly understood by householders that Public Shelters and Trenches are intended only for those who may be in the streets and cannot gain the safety of their own houses.

Persons in their own homes at the time of the alarm should on no account leave their houses during the raid.

B. W. SMITH, Chief Constable.
Controller.

John Buckle (Printers) Ltd., Theatre Plain, Gt. Yarmouth.

Air raid shelters under construction on Church Plain in 1939. Public sirens had been erected to give the population warning of imminent danger and during the war years there were 2,046 'alerts'. In addition to public shelters the Council provided over 600 Anderson shelters for householders to erect in their gardens while other homes used the indoor Morrison shelter.

The Links Battery on Gorleston Cliffs at the borough boundary. This battery was equipped with two 6-inch guns, the gun emplacements being connected by underground shelters and magazines. The rear approaches were covered by two adjoining pillboxes. Two searchlights stood on the cliff edge, either side of the guns. Later the armament was increased by two 40mm Bofors and a 25-pounder field gun. From 1941 until 1943 the battery was manned by the 325th Coast Battery, 514th Coast Regiment AA 2nd Corps seen here during gun drill removing the shell from its container (top) and carrying the shells to the gun floor (right).

Although the gun batteries had lost most of their original function early in the war when danger of invasion receded the Links Battery was kept operational until January 1945.

The scene at Vauxhall Station on Sunday 2 June 1940, parents waving goodbye to their children as the special 'evacuation' train pulls out of the station. On this Sunday over 47,000 children (3,700 from Yarmouth) were evacuated from 18 East Coast towns in 97 special trains.

First Aid Post and ARP personnel photographed in the gardens of Telegraph House (now Seafield Road) c1940. In the background is the SW corner of Melton Lodge (now Queen Elizabeth Court)

The 11th Battalion Norfolk Home Guard 'C' Company outside the Hospital School 1941.

The Home Guard, formed as the Local Defence Volunteers in May 1940, consisted of men between the ages of seventeen and sixty-five who for one reason or another were not engaged in military service. The only fitness requirement was that they should be 'capable of free movement'. In Yarmouth many men quickly volunteered and signed on at the Police Station, they were formed into three Companies, No.1 Company based at Church Road, Gorleston, No.2 company based at the Hospital School in the Market Place and No.3 Company at the Art School, later moved to St Peter's School. The Group Headquarters was at the Hospital School. In July they were renamed the Home Guard, training sessions held on Sunday and each weekday evening. The task of the Home Guard was to keep watch on the coast, public buildings, roads and railways for signs of enemy invaders and in Yarmouth they provided a guard for the town's two Gas Works and Beach Railway Station as well as manning the coastal battery on North Denes. Although not well equipped the Home Guard played an important role in local defence throughout the war, the Ormesby and Horsey platoons capturing a number of German airmen. The Home Guard was stood down on Sunday 3 December 1944 at a parade held at the Royal Aquarium where 90 officers and 1,849 other ranks received their final orders from their senior officer Lieutenant Colonel F.R.B. Haward.

Hill's Marine View on the corner of Euston Road after a direct hit during an air raid on 31 October 1940. Eight people were injured in this afternoon raid when four bombs were dropped from a single plane on Regent Road, the Eastern Star public house in Middle Market Road, Nettle Hill East and the last one on Hill's.

This raid happened at 11.30am on 10 September 1940 when four bombs were dropped at the south end of the town, one falling on open ground, one on the scenic railway at the Pleasure Beach and a third in a yard opposite the AFS station. The fourth bomb scored a direct hit on No 40 Harbord Crescent. The house was empty but the houses either side were completely wrecked and in one of these a young woman was killed. Another woman was killed in the other wrecked house. As well as the two fatalities there were five people injured in this raid and four other bombs failed to explode.

HRH The Duke of Kent during his visit to the town on 25 April 1941. The Duke is seen here with the Mayor (Mr E.R. Herman), the Chief Constable (Mr C.G. Box) and members of a demolition squad inspecting bomb damage in the Middlegate area.

The Angel Hotel in the Market Place was, from 1942, used as the British Restaurant where a nourishing meal could be obtained for 1s 1d, Soup 2d, Meat & Veg 7d, Sweet 3d and a Cup of Tea 1d. The hotel was demolished in 1958 and shops built on the site, one of which today is Dixons.

The network of rivers and broads were patrolled by the Broads Flotilla, Norfolk Division 2nd Corps. This flotilla of armed motor boats was operated by the Navy until 1941 and then taken over by the Army. On the large broads such as Hickling, holiday hire cruisers were moored in lines to act as a deterrent to sea planes attempting to land.

Members of the Fire Service gathered for a parade in the Market Place. Until August 1941 all fire fighting was under the control of the Chief Constable and carried out by the Auxiliary Fire Service made up from 350 full and part time firemen. The National Fire Service was then formed, the town becoming Sub Divisions 1 & 2 of Division B, No 13 Fire Force.

The AFS team based at Grouts Silk Factory in 1941. From left to right: R. Snowling, D. Brown, D. Jenkins, T. Haylett, F. Cox, G. Brown, S. Harrison.

The silk factory of Grout & Co. was damaged in an air raid on 1 February 1941 during which three people were killed and nine injured. Twelve high explosive bombs were dropped in a low level attack on an area from Kitchener Road to Middle Market Road. One bomb hit the South Mill of the factory and started a fire while other bombs ricocheted from the roadway, hitting other buildings close by.

Throughout the war the factory produced parachute silk and crepe bandages. From 1943, when the supply of silk from the far east stopped the parachute material was woven from the new man-made material, nylon. The site of the factory is now Sainsburys Supermarket in St Nicholas Road.

The remains of the 13th century Greyfriars cloisters after the air raids of April 1941. Historic buildings such as this were given temporary 'first aid' by the Ministry of Works in an attempt to save what was left. The two vaulted cloister bays which survived are today the only remains in England of any cloister of a Greyfriars or Franciscan Friary.

The remains of Reynolds Garage which stood at the corner of Apsley and Rodney Roads. This raid happened at 2.13pm on 27 February 1941 when a Junkers 88 aircraft dropped 13 high explosive bombs in a line east to west from Apsley Road to King Street.

These two photographs show the remains of the Seagull Garage in Queen's Road after the raid of 8 April 1941. The damage was caused by a parachute mine dropped at 5am. The garage was used as a station for the Special Constabulary, five of whom were killed.

The burnt out shell of the Parish Church of St Nicholas after the incendiary raid of 25 June 1942. In this raid over 1500 incendiary bombs were dropped from a great height over a wide area of the town, followed by eight high explosive bombs. Many large fires started resulting in damage to Lacons Brewery, the rear of shops in the Market Place, the Gas Works, Electricity Works and Docwra's Sweet Factory in Middlegate.

The Boys Brigade had been on duty as fire-watchers at the church but they were beaten by the size and intensity of the blaze. Within five minutes the church was well alight and 15 minutes later the spire collapsed. By morning only the outer shell of the building was left.

In the following days messages of sympathy were received from many places including Coventry, whose cathedral had suffered a similar fate a few months earlier in the war. It was to be 20 years before the parish church was rebuilt and in use again.

Lacons Brewery Stores, North Quay, was almost destroyed in the raid of 25 June 1942. Three people had been killed and 19 injured in this raid, described on the previous page. The barrel store was rebuilt after the war but was demolished in 1997 to make way for the Aldi Supermarket now standing on the same site.

Unexploded bombs caused great problems and dangers. This one, on South Quay 24 October 1942, is being excavated using a dewatering plant. The white building in the background belonged to J. & W. Stuart, net manufacturers (now the corner of Nottingham Way) and next to that are the bombed remains of the Ferry public house.

The scene at the corner of Alderson and Palgrave Road after a raid on 29 July 1942 when four high explosive bombs were dropped by a Dornier 217 on the residential area at the north end of the town. Other bombs fell on the Royal Avenue and Salisbury Road area.

Delf & Sons, Wholesale Grocers, 67 Middlegate Street. (These premises were at one time a public house known as the Tomlinson Arms.)

The gate across the road marks the boundary of the area controlled by the military as a training ground. Throughout 1942 and 1943 the bomb damaged area of the town between King Street and the South Quay was cordoned off and used by troops as a training area for street combat before they were posted overseas. Many of these men were billeted at Caister Camp and the Old Hall Camp at Caister.

An unexploded high explosive bomb recovered by the bomb disposal squad in Admiralty Road. This bomb was the only one dropped in a 3.40am raid on 5 June 1941 close to Johnson's Clothing factory.

A 4000lb bomb which failed to explode in Fredrick Road, Gorleston. This was one of three bombs dropped in an early morning raid on 12 June 1941. The Tramway public house received a direct hit, killing four people, the landlord and his family.

A slogan chalked on the boarded up window of Darn's fish shop in Howard Street North reads '*make sure your children shall not fight another war'*, a sentiment echoed by almost everyone in the town after four years of war, death and destruction.

Hundreds of bomb damaged properties such as this in Howard Street, George Street , Middlegate and the Rows were demolished after the war and the area cleared for new housing units built in the early 1950s. The medieval heart of the town was lost for ever.

Victory in Europe was announced on 8 May 1945 and celebrations took place country wide. Street parties were organised in many parts of the town, this one on 10 May took place in Burnt Lane, Gorleston and included residents of nearby Beccles Road. People provided whatever they could and the party was followed by dancing and singing in the street. Helping to organise this party was Mrs Jean Bennington (7th from right) with her mother and sister Dolly.

The Naval Bases

In 1939 the Royal navy established a series of shore bases to protect the vital East Coast Convoy Route, a shipping lane from the Firth of Forth to the Thames. Through this channel, less than a mile wide, convoys of up to sixty merchant ships would carry essential supplies of food and materials for the war effort. These convoys had to be protected from the German E-boats and mines and Great Yarmouth was one of the bases from which mine sweepers, motor torpedo boats, air sea rescue boats and salvage tugs operated throughout the war. Little has appeared in print about these naval activities, most of which were operational during the hours of darkness and cloaked in secrecy. The Yarmouth base, known by the overall name *HMS Watchful*, was originally set up with its headquarters at the Walrond Institute (formerly the Smack Boys Home) on the quayside. In July 1940 the base was upgraded and Admiral Sir E. Fullerton was in charge. The Institute was destroyed by an air raid on 18 February 1941 and the headquarters then moved to the Naval Hospital (the patients having been evacuated to Lancaster). This base (from 1942 commanded by Admiral Sir D. North) controlled all the naval operations in town and became a Naval Information Centre and Naval Administrative Headquarters for the remainder of the war.

The fishing season continued in 1939, providing much needed food for the country but after the fleet had been frequently attacked by the enemy the authorities decided to suspend all fishing for the duration of the war. Many fishermen volunteered for the Royal Naval Reserve and their boats, both trawlers and drifters, were converted for minesweeping and anti-submarine duties. The convoy route had to be swept daily for mines and during the early years of the war in the Yarmouth section of the route, known as 'E-Boat Alley', many thousands of tons of shipping were lost to mines and torpedoes. The naval bases established at Great Yarmouth had to provide support and protection for this vital sea route and at the height of the war 220 officers and over 2,200 ratings were based at the port.

At the evacuation of Dunkirk in 1940 two minesweeping trawlers (both sunk on arrival) and 13 minesweeping drifters from the port as well as the Gorleston lifeboat *Louise Stephens* took part. A shore base for minesweepers, *HMS Miranda*, was established in 1940 at the Fishwharf and this was home to 29 minesweeping trawlers and 13 other ships commanded by Captain Caspar Swinley DSO, DSC who made his headquarters in an old sailing barge, the *Mehalah*, moored at the Fishwharf. By 1944 purpose built mine sweepers were in service, replacing some of the older fishing craft that had been requisitioned at the beginning of the war and at Yarmouth there were 16 of these but still 33 drifters and trawlers.

HMS Midge was established in January 1941 at the southern end of the Fishwharf as a base for Motor Torpedo Boats (MTBs) and Motor Gun Boats (MGBs). The officers' quarters were at the Shadingfield Lodge and the MTB flotilla had 7 boats and there were two Motor Launch flotillas with 8 boats each. This base was part of a chain of Coastal Forces bases established along the east coast following the attacks on the East Coast convoys by German E-boats the previous year. Boats from Yarmouth, whose main purpose was to protect the convoys often operated far from their home base, off the Dutch coast. Another role for these boats was to land secret agents on the Dutch coast.

On the open land towards the harbour mouth were the naval fuel oil tanks and gunnery school. At the Nelson Monument a signal station was set up and a base for Naval Rescue Tugs and the Admiralty Salvage Dept., responsible for towing and repairing damaged ships, was set up at the ABC Wharf and the Nelson Garage (Pertwee & Back Ltd). The two rescue tugs based here were *Norman* (later renamed *Diversion*) and *Krooman*. The Naval Bomb Disposal team was based at the Wet Dock Tavern, a public house on Southgates Road.

The port also became an important Air Sea Rescue base, involving both military (RAF and naval) craft and the RNLI. At the height of their operations the base operated 13 High Speed Launches and 8 Rescue Motor Launches and became the most active air-sea rescue base in the world. The crews were billeted in private houses and the boats moored on the Gorleston side of the river, opposite the naval oil tanks. More airmen were landed at Yarmouth than at all the other east coast ASR bases put together and during the years of conflict over 800 airmen were saved by the station. Three rescue launches were lost in enemy action. This ASR base continued in use until the 1950's.

During the war years Yarmouth was an important Naval base which lost 28 boats (including 10 trawlers and drifters) and 195 personnel in the fight to win the war.

Motor Torpedo Boats moored in the harbour, part of the flotilla attached to *HMS Midge* based at the Fishwharf. In 1941 two flotillas of Motor Launches were stationed at Yarmouth. These boats had supercharged engines and superior armament to the previous MGBs but were still much slower than E-boats. In 1943 *Midge* had 53 boats under its command.

An MTB makes its way down river from its base at the Fishwharf. These boats worked in pairs when acting as convoy escorts, keeping station on the seaward side of the convoy, halfway along. If E-boats appeared they fired their 3-pounders (surplus guns from old warships) and machine guns and stood by to rescue survivors.

The remains of the WRNS hostel at the corner of Queen's Road and Nelson Road after the air raid on 18 March 1943. A single plane dropped six high explosive bombs, one of which was a direct hit on the hostel. 13 girls were rescued from the rubble, 27 injured and 8 killed. The WRNS were billeted in the Dolphin Hotel and Duncan Hall School in Albert Square after this.

Four high explosive bombs dropped in the grounds of the Naval Hospital during a raid on 24 July 1942, causing considerable damage over a wide area including the Royal Naval Barracks.

A 1200Kg bomb dropped at the Pleasure Beach 30 May 1942. This bomb was converted into a letter box by engineers at Pertwee & Back and then used at *HMS Watchful* for the remainder of the war. Today it stands outside the Maritime Museum.

A Gorleston based Air Sea Rescue launch on exercise to rescue a ditched airman.

Herbert Woods boatyard at Potter Heigham where ASR boats were constructed. In this picture two Harbour Defence Launches and four ASR Pinnaces are under construction. Other Broads boatyards to construct boats for the services were H. Percival at Horning and G. Bunn at Wroxham.

Two completed ASR pinnaces, 1327 and 1328, make their way down river from Herbert Woods to Yarmouth on their way to their respective bases.

Air Sea Rescue launch crew members led by FO Lindsay leaving their Cliff Hotel quarters in 1944. The Cliff Hotel was used as the Sergeants' and Officers' Mess.

Air Sea Rescue High Speed Launches at their Baker Street moorings. The base reached its maximum strength in 1943/44 when 14 boats operated from Gorleston. The base was maintained by the RAF after the war and finally closed in the early 1950s.

ACKNOWLEDGEMENTS

My thanks go to the many people who have helped to make this book possible, not only by supplying photographs and information but also for checking its accuracy. If any errors have crept in unnoticed it is now my fault. I also thank my wife Jan for her encouragement throughout and her help in selecting the final collection of images. These images have come from many different sources as listed below but special thanks must go to Alec McEwen, Tony Overill, Don Myhill and Neil Storey for allowing me to draw on their expertise and use some of their material. For the photograph on the front cover and the quote on the copyright page I am grateful to Mrs Jean Bennington. Photographs not listed below come from my own collection.

Neil Storey page 5, 7T, 19, 31T, 31T, 41,
Imperial War Museum page 39T, 39B, 40T, 44T.
St John Norfolk Archive page 40B.
Gordon Berry page 45B.
Tony Overill page 55T, 55B, 57B, 58T, 58B, 59T, 59B.
Mrs. J Bennington Front Cover and 52B

 This is the second book in a proposed series covering many different aspects of the history of Great Yarmouth and Gorleston, further titles will be published at regular intervals.

FURTHER READING

The Diary of the Norfolk Artillery 1853-1909 by J. Sancroft Holmes - Jarrolds 1909.

A History of the Yarmouth Battery 1569-1926 by Major M. Castle - Jarrolds 1927.

The Story of a North Sea Air Station by C. Snowden Gamble - Spearman 1967.

Fortification of East Anglia by P. Kent - Terence Dalton 1988.

Death From the Skies by R. Wyatt - Gliddon Books 1990.

Gt Yarmouth at War by C. Tooke & D. Scarles - Poppyland 1989.

Gt Yarmouth 1939-1946 by C. Box - 1946.

The Battle of the East Coast 1939-1945 by J. Foynes - 1994

Yarmouth Fortifications 1750-1960 by C. Rye - Yarmouth Archaeology Vols 1984 to 1988.

Although many of these books are now out of print copies should be available at Local Studies Libraries.